D1222478

World Issues

Terrorism

Stanley Weitzman

Chrysalis Education

WORLD ISSUES

ANIMAL RIGHTS
DRUGS
EQUAL OPPORTUNITIES
GENETIC ENGINEERING
GENOCIDE
HUMAN RIGHTS
POVERTY
RACISM
REFUGEES
TERRORISM

Distributed in the United States by
Smart Apple Media
1980 Lookout Drive, North Mankato, Minnesota 56003

ISBN 1-93198-390-9

The Library of Congress control number 2003102643

Editor: Clare Weaver
Editorial Manager: Joyce Bentley
Designer: Mark Whitchurch
Consultant: John Polley
Picture Researcher: Glass Onion Pictures

Printed in Hong Kong/China
10 9 8 7 6 5 4 3 2 1

Picture Acknowledgements
We wish to thank the following individuals and organizations for their help and
assistance, and for supplying material in their collections: Associated Press 32 (Marty
Lederhandler), 42 (DOD); Camera Press 5 middle (Scanfoto); Popperfoto *front cover*
(Reuters), 1 (Reuters), 3, 4–5 (Reuters), 6, 7, 10, 11, 15 (Reuters), 18 (Reuters), 19 (Reuters),
20, 21 (Reuters), 23 (Reuters), 24 (Reuters), 25, 26 (Reuters), 27 (Reuters), 28–29 (Reuters),
30 (Reuters), 31 (Reuters), 33 (AFP/Eggitt), 34, 36, 37 (Reuters), 38 (Reuters), 40 (Reuters),
41, 44, 45 (Reuters), 47 (Reuters); Rex Features 5 top, 5 bottom (Sipa), 9 (Mansell/
TimePix), 12 (Sipa), 13 (Sipa), 14, 16 (Sipa), 17 (Action Press), 22 (Sipa), 28 top (Sipa), 46
(Dennis Stone); Topham Picturepoint 8, 35 (Bob Daemmrich/ImageWorks), 39 (PA), 43
(AP). The pictures used in this book do not show the actual people named in the case
studies in the text.

CONTENTS

Daria's Story

For those who worked in the twin towers of the World Trade Center in New York City, Tuesday, September 11, 2001 began as just another ordinary day. Workers arrived at their offices, made themselves coffee, and opened their mail, unaware that they were about to be caught up in the worst terrorist attack in history. At 8:45 a.m., a hijacked passenger airliner, flown by suicidal terrorists, was deliberately crashed into the upper stories of the north tower, causing a massive explosion. Eighteen minutes later, another hijacked plane hit the south tower. Soon afterward, both towers collapsed, killing more than 2,800 people.

DARIA COARD WAS in the north tower when the plane hit. She and 30 others were in an elevator, going up. It stopped at the 88th floor. Nine passengers, including Daria, had just stepped out when they felt a massive jolt. The elevator, with the other passengers still inside, fell back down the shaft. She had no idea how far it fell or what happened to them.

Daria and her co-workers began running down the stairs in an effort to get out of the building. They had to step over dead bodies in the stairwell. One injured woman handed Daria her identification, asking Daria to tell her family that she loved them.

When they finally reached the ground floor, Daria ran to the entrance. She felt an explosion and was thrown beneath a jeep. Debris was falling all around. She was so scared she didn't want to come out from under the jeep. Eventually, a stranger persuaded her to come out. What she saw in the moments after that will stay with her for the rest of her life.

She saw a shoe under a car. Picking it up, she saw it contained a leg with nothing attached to it. There was an overturned buggy containing a crying baby, and a rescue worker with his arm and shoulder missing, screaming and running. Looking up, she saw a number of people jumping or falling out of the building. One couple held each other's hands as they jumped. Daria was almost too shocked to move, but she knew she had to save herself for the sake of her children.

For weeks after the incident, Daria could sleep for only three hours a night. The images of what she saw that day gave her nightmares. She had to walk with the aid of a cane because of an injury to her knee resulting from the explosion. Daria had her birthday on September 17th. Her mother called her in the morning to say how glad she was that she could celebrate her birthday instead of having to bury her today.

In the afternoon, she met up with some of her co-workers for the first time since the attack. They hugged and cried and talked about the friends they had lost. It was one birthday Daria would never forget.

Terrorism around the world

Daria and the other victims of the September 11th attack are among thousands of people worldwide whose lives have been affected by terrorism.

EUROPE
The Basque are a people living in northeastern Spain and southwestern France. For more than 40 years, Spain has suffered the violence of ETA, a terrorist group fighting for the creation of an independent Basque state. During that time, ETA has killed more than 800 people.

SOUTH AMERICA
Sendero Luminoso (Shining Path) is a terrorist organization that aims to destroy the political and economic system of Peru and replace it with a "peasant revolutionary regime." Since 1980, it has been responsible for more than 30,000 deaths.

MIDDLE EAST
Since Israel took over Palestinian lands in 1967, it has frequently been attacked by pro-Palestinian terrorist groups, including Fatah, Black September, Hamas, and Hezbollah. Attacks increased in 2002 following Israeli incursions into Palestinian settlements.

What Is Terrorism?

Terrorism is the use of violence against civilians in order to achieve political aims. The three key words in this definition are "violence," "civilians," and "political." Terrorism is always violent, which is what distinguishes terrorist groups from other kinds of organizations, such as political parties. A terrorist attack, unlike most military operations, deliberately targets civilians. Finally, terrorism is always political. Unlike criminal gangs, who are motivated by greed, terrorists attack in order to achieve some political goal, such as overthrowing a government.

A hooded gunman from the Palestinian terrorist group, Fatah, watches over a Palestinian demonstration in the West Bank city of Nablus in September, 2002.

ALTHOUGH MOST PEOPLE who study or write about terrorism would agree with the above definition, there is still no worldwide agreement on what terrorism is. In fact, most organizations whose activities fit this definition would deny they were terrorists. This is because the word terrorism is regarded by most people as something bad or negative—terrorists are usually seen as the enemy. Groups engaged in violent action to win power in their country are more likely to describe themselves as "freedom fighters" or "revolutionaries" than terrorists.

Just as violent groups will often deny they are terrorists, repressive governments often accuse opposition groups of terrorism, even if the rest of the world sees these groups as brave resistance fighters. Labeling such groups as terrorists helps to make any violent action by governments seem more justifiable.

Terrorists often accuse the governments they oppose of using terrorism in their attacks on them. However, governments tend to view terrorism as something that only nongovernment groups are capable of. For example, in its definition of terrorism, the US State Department describes those who perpetrate terrorism as "subnational groups or clandestine agents." It does not include governments within its definition. However, this view of terrorists is relatively recent. Throughout history, there have been governments that have used terrorism to enforce their authority. This is known as state terrorism.

A holy war

"We don't see ourselves as terrorists, because we don't believe in terrorism. We see ourselves as mujahideen [holy warriors] who fight a holy war for the people."

Sheikh Muhammad Hussein Fadlallah, spiritual leader of the Islamic terrorist group, Hezbollah.

John Hinckley, who attempted to assassinate president Ronald Reagan in 1981, is led away by police. (At his trial he was found not guilty for reasons of insanity.) He is not regarded as a terrorist since he did not have a political motive for the attack.

There is no universally agreed definition of terrorism. The problem is summed up by the phrase, "One man's terrorist is another man's freedom fighter." In this book, the word "terrorist" will be applied to any individuals, organizations, or governments that are engaged in violence against civilians for political aims. Whether those aims justify the violence committed in their name is up to the reader to judge.

DEBATE—Is terrorism an evil that everyone should fight?

- Yes. Terrorist actions can never be justified, no matter how seemingly worthy the cause.
- No. Terrorism is just a label we give to people and causes we happen to be against.

Has Terrorism Always Existed?

Terrorism has existed since the dawn of civilization. Before the 1800s, most terrorism was carried out by governments. The Roman emperor, Nero, used terror to maintain authority by ordering the execution of anyone suspected of plotting against him. In the 1400s, Spanish monarchs set up an Inquisition to cross-examine, torture, and execute subjects who were not sincere believers of the Catholic faith. Nonstate terrorism also existed. In 1605, a group of Catholics tried to overthrow the English government by blowing up the Houses of Parliament with gunpowder.

THE WORD "TERRORISM" was first used in 1795 by a British writer and politician called Edmund Burke. He used it to describe the policies of the French government of 1793–4. During this time, known as the Reign of Terror, the French government was trying ruthlessly to establish its authority following a revolution. Hundreds of people were executed for suspected counter-revolutionary activities, creating a climate of fear in the country.

What was "propaganda of the deed?"

In the 1850s, an Italian antimonarchist (someone opposed to rule by kings) called Carlo Pisacane, developed a theory of terrorism called "propaganda of the deed." It was Pisacane's belief that violent action was the only way of causing real change. "Ideas result from deeds, not the latter from the former…," he wrote. Pisacane's

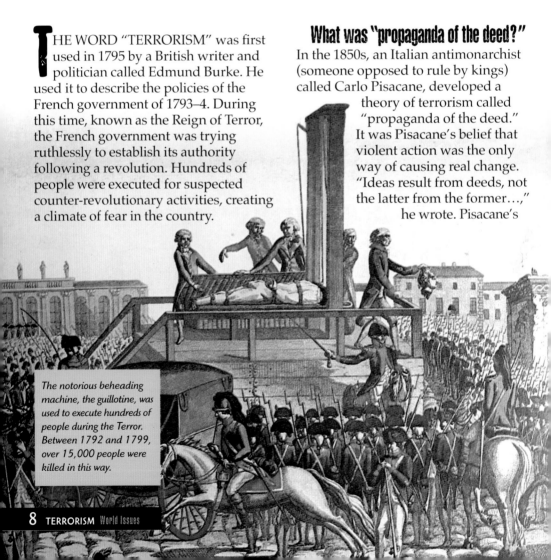

The notorious beheading machine, the guillotine, was used to execute hundreds of people during the Terror. Between 1792 and 1799, over 15,000 people were killed in this way.

theory inspired revolutionaries fighting against the Russian government in the 1870s. Groups such as Narodnaya Volya were among the first non-government organizations to be actually labeled terrorists.

The terrorist methods of the Russian revolutionaries influenced anarchist groups in Europe and the US, who carried out a string of assassinations between 1878 and about 1920. Their approach was also adopted by various groups fighting for freedom within the Ottoman Empire (a Turkish empire extending through southeastern Europe, western Asia, and the Middle East), such as the Macedonians, the Armenians, and the Bosnian Serbs.

Narodnaya Volya

Narodnaya Volya (meaning People's Will) was a group of Russian revolutionaries, founded in 1878, dedicated to the overthrow of the Russian tsar. In contrast with modern terrorists, Narodnaya Volya avoided killing innocent civilians. They targeted only senior members of the government, including the tsar himself, whom they assassinated in 1881. This success led to their downfall. The secret police hunted them down, and by 1883 every member had been executed.

What was totalitarian terrorism?

In the 1930s, a new and brutal version of state terrorism emerged in the form of totalitarian regimes—most notably the Soviet Union (a country formed from the territories of the Russian Empire) and Nazi Germany. In both countries, large numbers of political opponents were exiled, imprisoned, or killed, often on invented charges, in order to strengthen the ruling party's power.

Leon Czolgosz, pictured here in jail, was an anarchist terrorist who assassinated president William McKinley in 1901.

During the 1930s, the Soviet regime tried many thousands of people suspected of counter-revolutionary activities. The accused were forced to give false confessions of their guilt, and were then imprisoned or shot.

What's happened since the 1950s?

In the late 1940s and early 1950s, numerous countries in Asia, Africa, and the Middle East were controlled by European powers, such as Britain and France. Many of the native populations formed independence movements, some of which used terrorist methods. Groups such as the Fronte de Liberation Nationale (FLN) in Algeria, the Viet Minh of Vietnam, and the Jewish group Irgun in Palestine, successfully made use of terrorism to bring an end to colonial rule by the European powers.

Why was 1968 so important?

The year 1968 can be seen as a watershed in the history of terrorism. Starting in this year, the world experienced a major upsurge in terrorist violence. Groups seeking political change, or an end to oppression, began to use violence as a way of placing pressure on governments. Many terrorist groups began to seek support from sympathetic governments or organizations in other parts of the world. Attacks were often aimed at a global audience and terrorism became an international phenomenon.

1968 was also the year when the Western world was rocked by a wave of student protest movements, demonstrating against American military action in Vietnam and, more generally, against the capitalist system (the economic system based on free trade that operates in the West). A number of revolutionary terrorist groups emerged, such as the Red Brigades in Italy, the Weathermen in the US, and the Red Army Faction in West Germany. They carried out violent attacks throughout the 1970s and 1980s in the hope of bringing about political change.

What is fundamentalist terrorism?

Another milestone year in the history of terrorism was 1979, when a fundamentalist Islamic regime took power in Iran. Islamic fundamentalism is a form of Islam, which emphasizes a strict interpretation of the teachings laid down in the Muslim holy book, the Qur'an. The Iranian revolution inspired radical Muslims across the Islamic world to try to overthrow their governments and impose fundamentalist regimes in their own countries, often by means of terrorism. Islamic fundamentalists are also sworn enemies of Israel, and its supporters in the West—particularly the US. As a result, attacks on Israel increased and American interests also became targets of terrorist attack.

Since 1990, the revolutionary terrorism of the 1960s has faded in importance. The most significant terrorist force in the world today is Islamic fundamentalism. Terrorist organizations have become ever more global in scope, and more sophisticated and deadly in their methods. Some have become heavily involved with the drugs trade, and are barely distinguishable from criminal gangs. The most powerful organizations are highly secretive, made up of semi-independent groups, or cells, hidden within major cities throughout the world.

One of three hijacked planes is blown up in Jordan in 1970 by a Palestinian terrorist group, the Popular Front for the Liberation of Palestine.

Why Do People Become Terrorists?

There are many millions of people in today's world living under foreign or oppressive regimes, who long for freedom, or political or religious reform. Very few of them are terrorists. So, what kind of people turn to terrorism?

TERRORISTS ARE NOT necessarily the poorest or most desperate of people. They are often wealthy and well-educated. They are people whose whole lives are preoccupied with a particular cause. They live for the future, a time close at hand or far in the distance, when they will achieve their aims. In a terrorist's mind, violence is justifiable if it leads to a more perfect future.

For religious terrorists, this destiny has usually been prophesied, and will therefore happen. The Egyptian Islamic group, Gamat al-Islamiya, said of its opponents in 1996, "They plot and plan and God too plans, but the best of planners is God." Nonreligious terrorists can also be convinced of the ultimate success of their struggle. Leila Khaled, a Palestinian terrorist, wrote in 1973, "We shall win because we represent the wave of the future."

The terrorist Abu Nidal was responsible for the deaths of over 300 people in the 1970s and 1980s. In his case, the commitment to the cause of Palestinian liberation became an obsession with violence for its own sake.

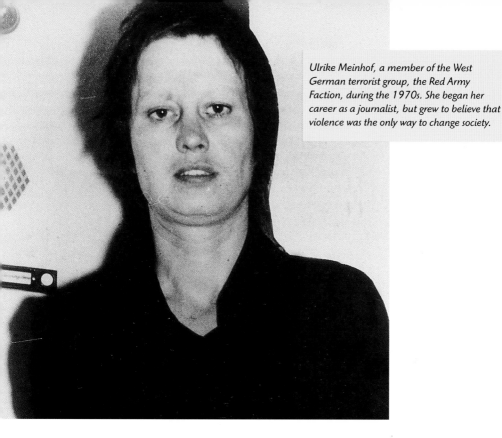

Ulrike Meinhof, a member of the West German terrorist group, the Red Army Faction, during the 1970s. She began her career as a journalist, but grew to believe that violence was the only way to change society.

Why do terrorists use violence?

Terrorists are driven by an impatience to achieve their goals. They have no trust in the power of words or the democratic process to bring about change. They believe that violence is the only effective way of changing the world. Maria Catarain of the Basque terrorist group Euzkadi to Askatasuna (ETA) said in the 1970s, "The only possibility we have of gaining our liberty is through violence."

For some terrorists, this faith in violent change can lead to an obsession with violence itself. An IRA member, Eamon Collins, noticed how his cousin Mickey became preoccupied with the details of the next killing to the exclusion of everything else. Many terrorists, including Michael Baumann of the Second of June Movement, Eamon Collins, and Susana Ronconi of the Red Army Faction, have described the great thrill they experience after carrying out an attack.

However, generally speaking, terrorists are not insane or uncontrollably violent. The most successful—and dangerous—terrorists are the ones who manage to combine their fervent belief in a cause with a professionalism in their operations. They choose their targets carefully for maximum impact. They are cautious and methodical in their planning, and technically highly competent.

"At the time, I felt the brutality of that action ... [But it] was a kind of excitement too because something had happened. The real thing [had] started now."

Silke Maier-Witt of the Red Army Faction, after murdering four bodyguards during the kidnapping of German industrialist Hans Martin Schleyer.

Tamil Tigers

The Liberation Tigers of Tamil Eelam (LTTE) aimed to create an independent nation for the Tamil community in northeast Sri Lanka. The LTTE, formed in 1976, combined terrorism with conventional warfare in its struggles with the Sri Lankan government. The LTTE has its base in northern Sri Lanka, and it controls most of the northern and eastern coastal areas. Since 1976, more than 64,000 people have died in the conflict. In December, 2001, the LTTE announced a ceasefire and began successful peace talks with the Sri Lankan government in late 2002. The LTTE has dropped its demand for an independent state, and plans to transform itself from a terrorist group into a political party.

What is nationalist terrorism?

Nationalist terrorism can occur when there is a group with a common ethnic identity who wish to form their own nation, or a people who were once an independent nation before their land was occupied by a conquering power.

Who are nationalist terrorists?

The Palestine Liberation Organization (PLO) aims to re-establish a Palestinian state on land currently occupied by Israel. Since it was founded in 1964, the PLO has spawned a number of terrorist groups, including the Popular Front for the Liberation of Palestine and al-Fatah, which have carried out frequent attacks on Israel in the years since 1968. In 1988, the PLO leader Yassir Arafat called off the terrorist campaign and accepted that Israel had a right to exist. This led to the first serious peace deal between the two sides, signed in 1993. This agreement granted the Palestinians limited self-government of territories in the West Bank and the Gaza Strip, as a step toward a fully independent Palestine. Two groups within the PLO left the organization in protest at this deal and continued their terrorist campaign. In 2000, Israel occupied Palestinian settlements in the West Bank and Gaza, provoking an uprising by the Palestinians. By 2002, the peace process remained under severe threat. The PLO failed to control the violence of radical Palestinians and Israel adopted an even more aggressive policy by bombing Palestinian territories.

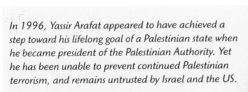

In 1996, Yassir Arafat appeared to have achieved a step toward his lifelong goal of a Palestinian state when he became president of the Palestinian Authority. Yet he has been unable to prevent continued Palestinian terrorism, and remains untrusted by Israel and the US.

Another nationalist terrorist organization is the Provisional Irish Republican Army (IRA), formed in 1968. The IRA wishes to bring an end to British rule in Ulster (Northern Ireland), and reunify all of Ireland as a Catholic country. Its fiercest opponents are the Protestant Unionist community of Northern Ireland, who want to remain part of Britain. For 25 years, the IRA attacked British military and Ulster police targets in Northern Ireland, as well as targets in mainland Britain. Since negotiations began with the British government in the early 1990s, there has been substantial progress toward peace, but mistrust remains between the two communities.

How do nationalists view violence?

Nationalist terrorist groups tend to be less inclined to kill large numbers of innocent civilians in their attacks than, for example, religious terrorists. This is because they are aware of the potential damage to their image within their own communities. Both the IRA and ETA send coded warnings before their bomb attacks to give police time to evacuate the area. When they do cause large-scale loss of life, they often publish messages of apology, as the IRA did after the bombing at Enniskillen in 1987, which killed 11 civilians and injured 63.

Have they achieved anything?

Nationalist terrorist groups are often more durable (long lasting) than other kinds of terrorist organizations. They usually have a strong base of support within their own communities, and their cause—national liberation—tends to attract widespread sympathy in the world at large, even if most people are repelled by their methods. Nationalist terrorist campaigns are more successful than other kinds of terrorism in bringing about tangible gains for the terrorists. They rarely attain their ultimate goal of independence, but Basques, Irish nationalists, Palestinians, Tamils and many others, have managed to achieve some level of self-government.

A mother leads her children past a wall daubed with pro-IRA graffiti in a Catholic area of Belfast in March, 2001. The specter of a return to terrorism continues to haunt Northern Ireland.

What is political terrorism?

Many terrorists are stirred to action because of a hatred of the values, or principles, of those in power, both in their country and around the world. There are two major kinds of political terrorist: left wing and right wing.

Left-wing groups support the idea of radical political or social reform. Many have been influenced by the writings of communist thinkers, such as Marx, Lenin, and Mao. They see the capitalist economic system as the major cause of inequality and poverty in the world and would like to bring about its violent overthrow.

Many left-wing groups emerged out of the wave of student riots in the late 1960s. These included the Red Brigades of Italy, the Red Army Faction of Germany, the Japanese Red Army, the Weathermen in the US, and Direct Action of France. Their most active period was during the 1970s and 1980s. By the early 1990s, many had either disbanded or ceased their activities. This was partially due to the success of government forces in breaking up their organizations, but also because of a general decline in support for radical left-wing causes.

In South America, left-wing groups, Sendero Luminoso in Peru (identified on page 5), and National Liberation Army (ELN) in Colombia, for example, have been more durable. This is partially because these groups have a lot of support among the poor rural population of their countries, but mostly because they have found a rich source of funding through their involvement in the drugs trade.

A police officer examines bloodstains on a Rome street at the scene of the assassination of Italian government official, Marco Biagi, in March, 2002. The killing marked a return to violence by the left-wing terrorist group, the Red Brigades.

A demonstration in Berlin by the neo-Nazi group, the National Democratic Party (NPD). The NPD has been linked to a string of violent attacks on immigrants and minority groups.

Right-wing groups wish to preserve traditional ways of life, which they see as under threat. They are usually fiercely patriotic, racist, and homophobic. In the US, right-wing groups are often associated with fundamentalist (very strict) Christian beliefs, for example, they are strongly opposed to abortion. In Europe, extreme nationalism is a far stronger factor than religion in the mindset of right-wing terrorists. German groups, such as the Nationaler Widerstand (Nationalist Resistance), Blood and Honor, and the British group Combat 18, are strongly influenced by the ideology of the Nazis. They are violently opposed to immigration and believe in forced repatriation (return of people from ethnic minorities to the countries of their ancestral origin).

Right-wing terrorist violence is often small scale, with little evidence of planning or organization. It typically takes the form of attacks on foreigners or members of ethnic minorities. In Berlin in 1998, there were 991 attacks on Jewish sites, including cemeteries, synagogues, and memorials. Black and Asian people in American and British cities have also suffered from right-wing terrorism in recent years.

Revolutionary organization 17 November

This left-wing Greek terrorist group was one of the most active terrorist organizations during the 1980s. Its name refers to the date of a student uprising in Athens in 1973 that was violently put down by the Greek government. Its main targets have been Greek politicians and officials. In July, 2002, Greek authorities finally caught up with 17 November, with the arrest of seven of its members.

What is religious terrorism?

Religious extremists sometimes turn to terrorism in an attempt to—as they see it—right the wrongs of the world, and do battle against the enemies of their faith. Because they see themselves as carrying out the will of God, religious terrorists tend to be less concerned about massacring people on a large scale, and the effect this might have on public opinion.

The most powerful form of religious terrorism in the world today is Islamic fundamentalism. The current upsurge in Islamic terrorism began after the Iranian revolution in 1979, when the fundamentalist leaders of Iran began trying to export their ideas. They funded terrorist groups in other Muslim countries, such as Hezbollah in Lebanon, in an attempt to topple the moderate governments and replace them with fundamentalist regimes.

The major focus of Islamic fundamentalist anger is Western, and especially American, interference in the Arab world. They see Western culture as a corrupting influence on Islamic society, and they are angered by the presence of American troops in Saudi Arabia. Fundamentalists believe American interest in the region is motivated mainly by its desire to protect access to oil. Fundamentalists, and many ordinary Muslims, are also angered by Israel's occupation of what they see as Palestinian lands.

Jewish terrorism has also been on the increase since the early 1980s. These groups were influenced by the sermons of the late Rabbi Meir Kahane, who preached a hatred of Arab people, and encouraged an aggressive attitude toward them. Jewish terrorists aim to expel all Arabs from Israel and, if necessary, kill those who refuse to leave. They have carried out many attacks on Palestinians, especially in the occupied territory of the West Bank.

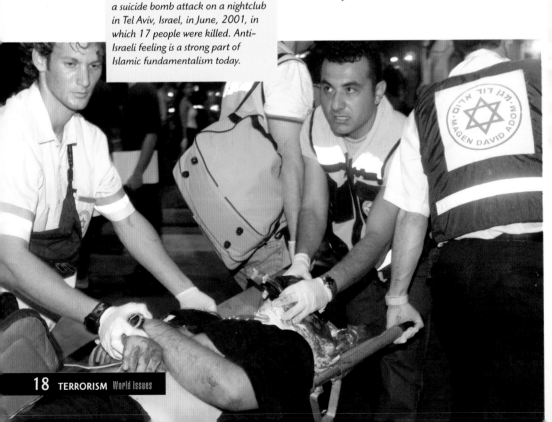

The wounded are evacuated following a suicide bomb attack on a nightclub in Tel Aviv, Israel, in June, 2001, in which 17 people were killed. Anti-Israeli feeling is a strong part of Islamic fundamentalism today.

Christian terrorist groups are to be found mainly in the US. They are political as well as religious, and are strongly associated with extreme right-wing racist views. The main source of their hatred is the American government and modern American culture, which they see as corrupt and antireligious. Groups such as the Christian Patriots and the Michigan Militia are miniature armies trained in survival and guerrilla warfare.

In April, 1995, the federal building in Oklahoma City was destroyed by a massive bomb planted by Timothy McVeigh, a member of a right-wing Christian militia group.

Al Qaeda

Al Qaeda (the Base) is the most powerful Islamic fundamentalist terror network in the world today. It considers its campaign against the US to be part of a war between Islam and the Christian and Jewish West. Al Qaeda was formed toward the end of 1980s as an umbrella organization offering funds and training to terrorist groups throughout the Arab world. It was involved in many of the major attacks of the recent past, including the 1993 bombing of the World Trade Center, the 1998 attacks on US embassies in Kenya and Tanzania, the attack on USS *Cole* in 2000, and the September 11th attacks on New York and Washington D.C. Its bases in Afghanistan were severely damaged by US–led forces in late 2001. However, al Qaeda has since regrouped, and was suspected of involvement in the attack on a Bali nightclub in October, 2002.

DEBATE—Can anyone become a terrorist, if circumstances drive them to it?

- Yes. Any person faced with the loss of their culture, their freedom, their home, can become a terrorist.

- No. Not every oppressed person turns to violence. It depends on a person's character.

How Do Terrorists Use The Media?

One of terrorism's main goals is to attract publicity for its cause, and terrorists rely on the world's media to provide that publicity. For their part, the media have always been willing to provide coverage of terrorism. This is because terrorist attacks are by their nature dramatic, and they provide exactly the kind of stories that boost audience figures for news channels and increase sales of newspapers.

TERRORIST ATTACKS ARE newsworthy, firstly, because they have a political aspect: the grievances of terrorists and government responses to terrorism can be analyzed and debated in detail. Secondly, they have a human aspect: terrorist attacks can result in death, injury, bereavement, as well as miraculous escapes. Kidnappings or hijacks can be especially tense, as the world waits to discover the outcome of a siege or a negotiation.

British newspapers use strong language to condemn the IRA assassination of the naval commander and statesman, Lord Mountbatten, in 1979.

DEBATE—Should the media stop reporting terrorist attacks?

- Yes. As Margaret Thatcher said, this would starve terrorists of the "oxygen of publicity," and terrorist attacks would stop.
- No. The media's duty is to report the news. To stop reporting on terrorism amounts to censorship.

What is the role of the media?

At times the media, in their desire for a story, have allowed themselves to become manipulated by the terrorists. In 1985, TWA flight 847 was hijacked by Hezbollah, and 39 Americans were flown to Beirut and held hostage there. In the days that followed, the TV networks placed massive pressure on the government by their in-depth coverage of the hostages' plight. This media-led campaign was a significant factor in persuading the government to negotiate with the terrorists.

Should the media be censored?

In October, 2002, when Chechen terrorists seized control of a Moscow theater, taking 800 people hostage, the Russian media inevitably took a close interest in the affair. The Russian government banned the media from reporting statements by the terrorists. One TV station, Moskoviya, was closed down for doing so. The media were even told not to make live broadcasts from the theater. Journalists complained that this amounted to censorship.

Bombing in Bali

There is a trend in terrorism toward large-scale, spectacular attacks inflicting high numbers of casualties. This may partially be because, in a time of increasing terrorist violence, smaller attacks no longer have such a power to shock, and therefore will attract less media coverage. An example of this was the October, 2002 attack on the Sari nightclub in the popular tourist resort of Kuta Beach, Bali, which killed over 180 people. The attack was blamed on local Islamic terrorists with possible links to al Qaeda.

Some politicians, such as Margaret Thatcher and Benjamin Netanyahu (a former Israeli prime minister), have argued that if terrorist attacks were not reported, then terrorism would soon cease. Netanyahu said "unreported, terrorist acts would be like [a] ... tree falling in the silent forest." However, Lawrence K. Grossman, president of NBC News, defends TV coverage, saying, "I have seen no evidence that audiences are ever taken in by the propaganda of terrorists who have blackmailed their way on to the television screen."

A still from a video showing Saudi–born terrorist Osama bin Laden (left) in conversation with a colleague. The video, released in December, 2001, shows them talking about their delight at the success of the September 11th attacks. The video, like several others featuring bin Laden, was widely broadcast; bin Laden uses the media in this way to reach out to his supporters and recruit new people to his cause.

How Do Terrorists Operate?

Terrorist groups are usually too weak to have any hope of toppling a government without help from others. Their attacks are therefore aimed at attracting recognition and support to their cause, both within their country and abroad. By applying pressure to an enemy government's weak points, they hope to provoke a general revolt that may bring about its collapse.

THERE ARE THREE principal aims that lie behind most terrorist attacks. The first of these is to attract maximum publicity for their cause.

Why is publicity crucial?

Terrorists select their targets with publicity in mind, attacking high-profile locations, such as financial or commercial districts of major cities. Whenever possible, they will opt for the dramatic or spectacular, such as a hijacking, or the kidnapping or assassination of a famous person. For terrorists involved in a hijacking, the publicity they attract is always the most important aspect of the operation. The fulfilment of their demands, such as prisoner releases, is simply a bonus.

How does demoralization work?

The second aim is to demoralize the enemy government and its supporters by creating a climate of fear and insecurity. This is achieved by timing attacks for maximum surprise and making use of any weaknesses in a country's security systems. In this way, people's faith in a government's ability to protect them from attack is undermined. By these means, terrorists hope to present an image of an invincible force that can strike anywhere, any time.

On September 11th, 2001, hijacked planes were deliberately flown into high profile buildings. The attacks purposefully targeted the symbols of America's financial power (the World Trade Center in New York) and its military might (the Pentagon in Washington D.C.). This was a clear example of a terrorist attack that aimed to demoralize or strike fear into the heart of an enemy country.

Carlos Marighela, the Brazilian terrorist and author, who wrote Mini-manual of the Urban Guerrilla (1969), was the first great strategist of modern terrorism.

A glass house

One of the first to articulate the third aim of terrorist attacks (provocation) was Menachem Begin, the leader of the Jewish terrorist group, Irgun, which launched attacks against British interests in Palestine in the late 1940s.

He wrote: "We knew that Eretz Yisrael [the land of Israel], in consequence of the revolt, resembled a glass house. The world was looking into it with ever-increasing interest and could see most of what was happening inside... Arms were our weapons of attack; the transparency of the 'glass' was our shield of defense."

Source: The Revolt: Story of the Irgun by Steimatzky

The National Liberation Army (ELN) of Colombia seek to demoralize the government by kidnapping, hijacking, and bombing.

Why is provocation used?

The third aim of terrorist attacks is to provoke the enemy government into violent acts of suppression. With such behavior, a government loses support and arouses sympathy for the terrorists' cause. An example of the successful use of this tactic was the FLN campaign to liberate Algeria from French rule in the 1950s. Their bombs provoked a violent reaction from the French authorities, who treated all those not of European origin as terrorist suspects, thereby alienating the entire native population.

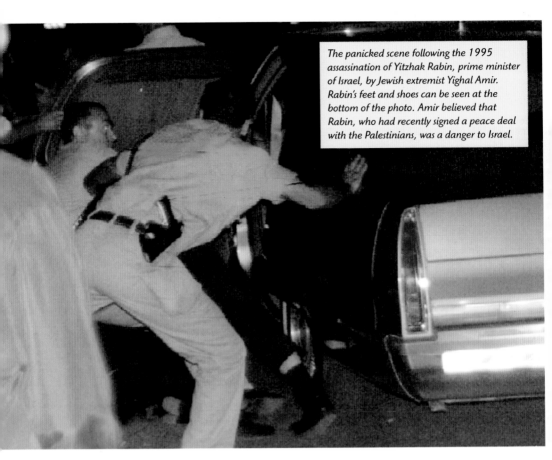

The panicked scene following the 1995 assassination of Yitzhak Rabin, prime minister of Israel, by Jewish extremist Yighal Amir. Rabin's feet and shoes can be seen at the bottom of the photo. Amir believed that Rabin, who had recently signed a peace deal with the Palestinians, was a danger to Israel.

What are the tactics of terror?

Terrorists choose their methods carefully in order to apply maximum pressure and discomfort to their enemies. They can choose to destroy property, kill or capture selected individuals, or imprison or massacre large numbers of people.

Why is hostage-taking so effective?

A common form of terrorism is hostage-taking. This can range from the kidnapping of a well-known person, to the hijacking of a commercial airplane. The advantage of this kind of operation is that it stretches out the terrorists' time in the media spotlight. It is also less likely to alienate potential supporters than straightforward killing, and appears to place the responsibility for the life or death of hostages on the shoulders of the enemy. By forcing the enemy to negotiate with them, hostage-taking can give the terrorists—for a brief time at least—a semblance (outward appearance) of power to rival governments.

What is assassination?

The targeted killing of government members and other powerful figures—assassination—is a typical ploy of left-wing terrorists. This is because they tend to be more concerned about their image among their supporters. They like to show they are not blind killers, but are selective in whom they choose to kill. For example, in 1977, the Red Army Faction kidnapped and murdered the rich businessman, Hans Martin Schleyer. In the following year, the senior Italian politician, Aldo Moro, was kidnapped and murdered by the Red Brigades.

Who uses bombing?

Terrorists with fewer concerns about their public image may use large bombs, powerful enough to destroy a building or a shopping center. These are usually concealed within a vehicle and detonated by remote control. An example of this was the bomb attack in August, 1998 in Omagh, Northern Ireland by a terrorist group called the Real IRA. The bomb went off in a busy shopping street, killing 28 people.

Al Qaeda are known for carefully coordinated, large-scale attacks. In August, 1998, al Qaeda members detonated a car bomb outside the US embassy in Nairobi, Kenya, killing 234 and injuring 5,000.

A suicide bomb attack

On June 18, 2002, Mohammed al-Ghoul, a 22-year-old Palestinian student, boarded a bus in Jerusalem. It was the morning rush hour and the bus was packed with commuters, students, and children. Inside the bus, al-Ghoul detonated the nail bomb strapped around his body. He killed 20 people including himself, and caused terrible injuries to many more.

What is suicide bombing?

Since the 1980s, a new weapon has entered the terrorists' armory: the suicide bomber. Suicide is forbidden by Islamic law, but this has not prevented many young Muslims from volunteering for "self-martyrdom" by blowing themselves up in crowded places. Unlike a remote-controlled bomb attack, suicide bombers are able to control the exact positioning and timing of the blast in order to inflict maximum casualties. This has been a tactic particularly used by Palestinian terrorists hoping to increase the pressure on Israel to pull out of the occupied territories.

How is money and support raised?

Terrorist groups raise money in many different ways. Some groups are supported by governments who are sympathetic to their cause. Others are involved in the drugs trade and other forms of organized crime.

How does illegal fundraising work?

Each terrorist group finds its own ways of supporting its activities. During its history, the IRA has received funds from sympathetic groups in the US, as well as weapons and training from the PLO and Libya. ETA is funded by Basque supporters and a mixture of drug smuggling, kidnap ransoms, and the proceeds of robberies. Right-wing terrorist groups in the US sometimes raise money by printing counterfeit money. Other common methods include money laundering (passing illegally acquired money through a legitimate bank account to disguise its origins) and loan-sharking (lending money at very high rates of interest).

The offices of the Holy Land Foundation for Relief and Development, in Richardson, Texas. The company was accused by the government of channeling funds to the Palestinian terrorist group, Hamas, and in December, 2001, its assets were frozen.

What are the legal methods?

Terrorists also raise money in legal ways, through charities, donations from sympathetic businesses, and by taxing their supporters. Shining Path in Peru charges rural businesses and individuals in areas under its control a "war tax." The Abu Nidal Organization, a Palestinian terrorist organization, earns much of its money legitimately through the interest earned on millions of dollars it holds in bank accounts in Switzerland, Austria, and Spain. Al Qaeda is partially financed by businesses owned by its leader, Osama bin Laden, including a large construction company in Sudan.

Islamic terrorist groups benefit from the Muslim custom of making regular charitable donations, known as *zeketh*. During Friday sermons at mosques, imams (preachers) will often ask the congregation to donate their money to Islamic charities. Together, Islamic charities raise billions of dollars each year. Most of these funds go to good causes, but some reach extremist organizations.

The Palestinian Hamas group raises tens of millions of dollars every year through a network of charities based in the occupied territories (West Bank and Gaza), Europe, and the US. Al Qaeda also raises a lot of its money through charities, some of which are genuine, but have been infiltrated by al Qaeda members. Others are merely front organizations that hide the real purpose of the funds.

Gerry Adams, president of Sinn Fein—the IRA's political wing—on a fundraising trip to New York in November, 2002. Irish American groups have been a key source of funds for the IRA in the past.

The *hawala*

Many Islamic terrorist groups use an underground banking system, known as the *hawala*, as a way of transferring money in secrecy. This system uses no contracts or printed records, and is based purely on trust. People can deposit or withdraw funds, or send them from one bank account to another, with a simple telephone call. Because there is no paper or electronic evidence of transactions, the *hawala* is almost impossible for counter-terrorism forces to monitor. *Hawala* banking systems have operated in South Asia and the Middle East for many generations and are therefore difficult to shut down. *Hawalas* have existed in the US since the 1980s.

What is state-sponsored terrorism?

Terrorists are sometimes given financial and other support by governments, particularly when they have a common enemy. This enables terrorists to mount ambitious operations they could not fund by themselves, and it allows countries to inflict damage on their enemies without having to risk open warfare.

State sponsorship of terrorism was a common policy of governments during the Cold War (1945–90), a period of hostility between the communist Soviet Union and its allies, and the capitalist West. During this period, left-wing and nationalist groups like the Red Brigades, the Red Army Faction, the Japanese Red Army, ETA, the PLO, and the National Liberation Army (of Bolivia), were given arms and funding by the Soviet Union or its allies. The American government, in similar fashion, gave support and training to terrorist groups opposing left-wing regimes in countries like Cuba, Guatemala, Argentina, Chile, and Vietnam.

Iranian women at a demonstration in support of Ayatollah Khomeini, the leading figure in Iran's 1979 Islamic fundamentalist revolution. Once in power, Khomeini tried to spread the revolution by funding terrorist groups in Lebanon, Egypt, Saudi Arabia, Jordan, and Algeria.

The wreckage of Pan Am flight 103 in a field near Lockerbie, Scotland, in December, 1988. The Libyan government was strongly suspected of involvement in the bombing, which killed 270 people.

Iraq

Saddam Hussein's Iraq (1978–2003) provided bases, training camps, and other kinds of support to terrorist groups fighting its neighboring states of Turkey and Iran. It also supported Palestinian groups fighting the Israelis. There were rumors of links between Iraq and al Qaeda, and even of Iraq's involvement in the attacks of September 11th, but so far, nothing has been proved.

What happened after 1990?

When the Cold War ended, most state sponsorship of terrorism also ceased. According to the US State Department, there are currently six major state sponsors of terror. They are Cuba, Iran, Libya, North Korea, Sudan, and Syria. However, there is little evidence to support the inclusion of Cuba, Libya, and North Korea in this list. Both Cuba and Libya have sponsored terrorist groups in the past, but have since distanced themselves from terrorism. North Korea has not been firmly linked to a terrorist attack since 1987.

Iran is probably the world's most active state sponsor of terrorism, providing funding, weapons, training, and safe haven to a number of terrorist groups based in the Middle East and elsewhere. Terrorist groups that benefit from Iran's support include Hezbollah in Lebanon, and Hamas and Palestinian Islamic Jihad in the Israeli-occupied territories. It also supports the Kurdistan Workers' Party, a non-Islamic nationalist group fighting against Turkey for an independent Kurdistan.

Syria, like Iran, supports Hezbollah, and has provided training, weapons, and a safe haven to both nationalist and religious Palestinian terrorist groups. Between 1980 and 1998, Syria was the base of operations for the Kurdistan Workers' Party. Since 1993, the fundamentalist regime in Sudan has, at certain periods, provided sanctuary for terrorist groups such as al Qaeda, the Abu Nidal Organization, and Egyptian Islamic Jihad, and has let them use Sudan as a base from which to carry out operations.

How are terrorism and crime linked?

Since the end of the Cold War, and the decline in state sponsorship of terrorism, many terrorist organizations have turned to crime, and especially drug smuggling, as a source of finance. This has led to a growing link between terrorist groups and international crime gangs. These are organizations that are structured like ordinary businesses, but they trade in illegal products, such as drugs, stolen goods, pirated CDs, counterfeit money, gambling, prostitution, and pornography. They are not political like terrorist groups, but terrorists and crime gangs find they can help each other in different ways by working together.

A cargo of heroin and morphine is captured from Iranian drug smugglers by Pakistani police in January, 2002. The drugs had an estimated street value of over half a billion dollars. Much of this may well have been used to fund terrorist activities.

Drugs and terrorism in Colombia

The Revolutionary Armed Forces of Colombia (FARC), a Colombian left-wing terrorist group, collects taxes from the farmers who grow coca (the crop from which cocaine is derived) on the land it controls. Some experts believe that the terrorist group forces farmers to grow coca. It also charges money for protecting the laboratories where the cocaine is produced, and the secret airstrips for the airplanes that transport the drugs. FARC also makes money on local sales of cocaine.

What is narcoterrorism?

The drugs trade is now the largest source of funding for terrorism worldwide. The link between terrorism and drugs is known as "narcoterrorism." In return for money, terrorist groups help drug gangs in different ways. For example, terrorist groups fighting for an independent Kosovo—especially the Kosovo Liberation Army (KLA)—have helped drug gangs in Albania by laundering their funds through their bank accounts. For this service, Kosovan terrorist groups were paid approximately 225 million dollars between 1996 and 1999. These terrorist groups also helped drug gangs by transporting drugs for them. In 1998 alone, the KLA helped to transport 2 billion dollars-worth of drugs into Europe.

The Islamic Movement of Uzbekistan (IMU) is a religious terrorist group fighting for an Islamic fundamentalist revolution in Uzbekistan. It funds its activities by helping in the transportation of heroin from Afghanistan, through the areas of Uzbekistan under its control, to Russia and Europe. This is despite the fact that Islamic law forbids the use or sale of drugs. Afghanistan is the world's largest producer of heroin, and about 70 percent of its total produce passes through Uzbekistan. In this case, the IMU's terrorist activities help to keep the country unstable, which makes it easier to continue with this profitable trade.

A suspected member of the Algerian terrorist organization the Groupe Islamique Armé (GIA) is arrested by Belgian police in March, 2002. The GIA is involved in extortion, currency counterfeiting, and money laundering.

How Does Terrorism Affect People?

Terrorism, by its nature, is a deeply shocking event for people to live through. Unlike soldiers in battle, victims of terrorism are usually taken by surprise and are not mentally prepared for an attack on themselves or their families. Those who survive an attack may have to face further challenges beyond the immediate shock, such as disability, disfigurement, or bereavement. They may suffer in the long term from fear, guilt, anger, and depression. Victims of terrorism often face years of traumatic memories about their ordeal.

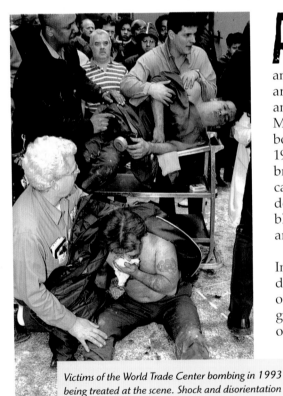

Victims of the World Trade Center bombing in 1993 being treated at the scene. Shock and disorientation are usually the first reactions to a terrorist attack.

AT THE MOMENT of a terrorist attack, people can react in different ways. Some can think very clearly and react to save themselves and those around them. Others may be stunned and lose sensation in their bodies. Una McGirk was a victim of the Omagh bombing in Northern Ireland in August, 1998. She heard the explosion, and was briefly knocked unconscious. When she came to, she got up and began walking down the street. She was drenched in blood, with severe wounds to her face, arms, legs, and torso—yet felt no pain.

In the days and weeks following a disaster, people can experience a variety of emotions including numbness, denial, grief, anger, and hopelessness. For others, the only alternative is to continue as normal. Gabriel Torres and his wife went ahead with the baptism of their two-year-old son, just days after Gabriel's narrow escape from the World Trade Center attack on September 11, 2001.

Living in the shadow of the suicide bomber

During the Palestinian *intifada* (uprising) that began in 2000, Israelis had to cope every day with the fear and anger that resulted from being the focus of a terrorist campaign. Each new suicide bombing caused yet more deaths, injuries, and bereavements. The Israeli novelist David Grossman wrote "There is not an Israeli who does not feel that his life is in danger." He described the scene in a restaurant in Jerusalem:

"I'm the only customer in the restaurant, which, until a few months ago, was generally packed around the clock. A few shoppers scurry past, their expressions indicating that they would rather be at home. They look from one side to another, constantly checking their surroundings. Any of the people nearby could be their murderer."

Source: British newspaper, The Guardian, April 2, 2002

Surviving the Oklahoma City bombing

"The unique characteristic of a terrorist act is that it is mainly a crime of belief... It is not a crime against a specific person, but rather against a government, a group of people, or an ideology... On the one hand, there was some comfort in the knowledge that there was no specific intent to harm each of us individually. On the other hand, we were angry that it did not matter to McVeigh who was killed or injured, because to him, we were totally expendable."

Susan Urbach, survivor of the bomb attack by Timothy McVeigh on the Oklahoma Federal Building in April, 1995.

Former hostage John McCarthy arriving back in Britain in August, 1991. McCarthy was held captive in Lebanon for five years by Hezbollah.

What Is The Future Of Terrorism?

Since the first hijackings in the late 1960s — when terrorists deliberately set out to grab the attention of the world — terrorism has become an international phenomenon. The victims of terrorism are no longer limited to citizens of enemy countries. In the September 11th attacks, citizens of around 60 countries died. The issues that drive terrorism today, such as religious fundamentalism and hatred of the West, cross national boundaries. Even those fighting an occupying government for the right to form an independent nation increasingly rely on the support of sympathetic groups in other countries.

TODAY, THE WORLD has become even more closely linked by a process known as globalization. Trade and travel has become easier and cheaper. Information can be shared over the Internet. The global banking system allows businesses and individuals to switch money between accounts almost anywhere in the world in a matter of minutes.

International terrorist organizations have taken advantage of globalization and advances in communications technology. It has allowed al Qaeda operatives (members) to communicate with and move funds between its cells, in 60 different countries across the Middle East, Asia, Europe, and North America. They make use of the Internet, encryption software (a means of coding messages), and the latest information technology. Globalization has also meant that very small extremist groups or individuals, such as right-wing groups in Europe and the US, can make a big impact because they have easier access to sophisticated weaponry.

Theodore Kaczynski—known as the Unabomber—being led into court in January, 1998. Over a 17-year period, Kaczynski detonated 16 homemade bombs, killing three people and injuring 23. Nowadays, it is easier for small groups or individuals to wage terrorist campaigns.

The Internet has made the transfer of information between terrorist groups or cells much easier and quicker.

Why use cyberterrorism?

Computers are another area vulnerable to international terrorist attack. The Western world is increasingly dependent on computers for the normal functioning of businesses and services. Cyberterrorism is the name given to terrorist attacks on computer systems. Such an attack, by means of a computer virus or an electromagnetic bomb, could cause chaos in a country's transportation system, its hospitals, and police. Cyberterrorists can also hack into the computer networks of enemy governments, destroying information, or accessing secret files.

Terrorist groups might choose cyberterrorism firstly because it is inexpensive. It can be carried out from a remote location in another country, and therefore does not entail the risk of crossing borders. Online attackers can easily hide their identity by pretending to be someone else. Cyberterrorism is a tempting way of attacking enemy governments in an area where they are vulnerable, creating fear and potentially large financial losses. The Tamil Tigers have launched several online attacks against the Sri Lankan government.

Some American government officials believe al Qaeda has been training its operatives in cyberterrorist techniques. Evidence has been found in its Afghanistan bases to suggest that al Qaeda has been looking closely at the systems that control American energy supplies, water distribution, and communication networks.

What are weapons of mass destruction?

Weapons of mass destruction (WMD) is the collective name for biological, chemical, and nuclear weapons. If terrorist groups get hold of these kinds of weapons, the potential destruction could be devastating.

DEBATE—In 20 years' time, will terrorists still be fighting for the same causes as those of today?

* Yes. Religious fundamentalism, world poverty, and the oppression of ethnic minorities will still be with us in 20 years, and so will the terrorism that is born from these issues.
* No. In the future, new issues will arise to provoke terrorism, such as environmentalism, globalization and animal welfare.

Biological weapons are weapons used to deliver deadly bacteria, such as smallpox, anthrax, or bubonic plague, to harm or kill people. Methods of delivery can vary from bombs or missiles to infected animals. An anthrax or smallpox terrorist attack on a city would be difficult, as the bacteria are not easy to acquire, weaponize (modify to make more deadly), or deliver effectively. The biggest threat would be releasing them into enclosed areas, such as an office ventilation system or a subway carriage. In October, 2002, a biological attack was launched via the US postal service. Anonymous letters containing anthrax spores (a dormant form of the bacteria) were sent to the offices of several senators and senior media figures. Five people died in the campaign.

This letter, laced with the deadly bacteria anthrax, was sent to a senator in October, 2001.

4TH GRADE
GREENDALE SCHOOL
FRANKLIN PARK NJ 08852

SENATOR DASCHLE
509 HART SENATE OFFICE
BUILDING
WASHINGTON D.C. 2051

20510/4103

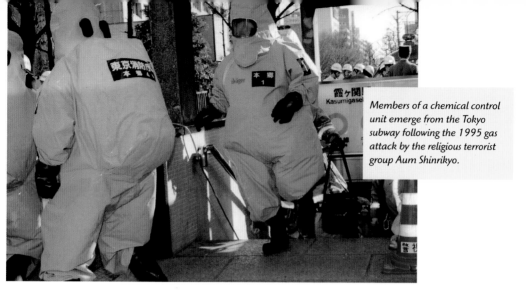

Members of a chemical control unit emerge from the Tokyo subway following the 1995 gas attack by the religious terrorist group Aum Shinrikyo.

Chemical weapons deliver toxic (poisonous) substances, such as chlorine gas or mustard gas. One of the most dangerous chemical weapons is sarin—a colorless, odorless nerve gas. It disrupts the nervous system, overstimulating muscles and vital organs. In 1995, sarin was used in diluted form in an attack on the Tokyo subway in Japan. Twelve people were killed and thousands were injured. It has also been reported that al Qaeda tried to make chemical weapons including sarin and VX, another deadly nerve agent.

Nuclear weapons are bombs with massive explosive power, caused by nuclear fission—a process that involves splitting the nuclei (central parts) of atoms into smaller particles. When the nuclei of certain materials, such as enriched uranium or plutonium, undergo this process in a chain reaction, the energy released could destroy a city. Those not killed by the explosion may then be injured or killed by radiation sickness, caused by the cloud of radioactive dust left behind by nuclear explosions, known as fallout.

Dirty bombs

A "dirty bomb" is the name commonly used for a radiological weapon. This is a conventional explosive packed with radioactive material, which scatters when the bomb goes off. Dirty bombs are much less destructive than nuclear weapons, but easier to build, and therefore a more likely threat. Although the explosion would not kill many more than a conventional bomb, the panic caused by the threat of radiation sickness could paralyze a large town or city.

Nuclear weapons are fortunately very difficult to make. They require specialist knowledge and equipment, and the raw material is very rare. The most likely way in which a terrorist group might acquire a nuclear weapon is by stealing one from the poorly guarded stockpile that belonged to the former Soviet Union. Between 1999 and 2002, Russian authorities claim to have broken up hundreds of nuclear-material smuggling operations.

Can Terrorism Be Stopped?

How should governments deal with the threat from terrorists? One way is to sit down and talk with them. Negotiating with violent groups may seem distasteful. It may appear to give violent people a status and a legitimacy, which they don't deserve. Yet many governments have held talks with terrorists, even if they do not admit to it in public.

NATIONALISTS HAVE BEEN more successful than other kinds of terrorist groups in bringing governments to the negotiating table. This may be because, unlike many political and religious groups, nationalist groups tend to have clearly defined and achievable goals, such as the desire to govern themselves. They are also usually well-supported by a significant minority in the country where they are based, and by sympathetic governments and groups in other countries. This makes their claims harder to ignore.

Israel, while known for its generally tough stance on pro-Palestinian and Islamic terrorism, has occasionally entered into negotiations or offered concessions to terrorists. One notable occasion followed the hijacking of a TWA flight in 1985. Thirty-nine Americans were among those held hostage, and the US government pressurized Israel into releasing several hundred imprisoned members of Hezbollah. Of more lasting significance was the peace deal signed by Israel and the PLO in 1993, which followed several weeks of secret negotiations between the two sides.

Former president Bill Clinton encourages Israeli prime minister Yitzhak Rabin (left) and PLO chairman Yassir Arafat to shake hands following the signing of a peace accord by the two leaders in 1993.

The Northern Ireland peace process

In 1994, after several years of secret negotiations between the IRA and the British government, the IRA announced a ceasefire. The British government declared that the IRA could join talks on the future of Northern Ireland if it permanently renounced violence. This led, in 1998, to the Good Friday Agreement, which shifted power from the British government to a new Northern Ireland assembly with representatives from both sides of the community. However, the road to peace is rarely straightforward—in October, 2002, the assembly was suspended and British rule reimposed, following allegations that the IRA was still involved in terrorist activities.

Does negotiation work?

Negotiating with terrorists can be problematic. If handled badly, negotiations can give people the impression that a government is weak or willing to be blackmailed by violence. Concessions can appear to devalue the sacrifices made by those who have fought against terrorism. It is often equally difficult for terrorists to sit down and talk with those they have always regarded as the enemy.

Nevertheless, if the timing is right, negotiations can sometimes produce dramatic results. In 2002, after 26 years of violence, the Sri Lankan government and the Tamil terrorist group, LTTE, began peace negotiations. By September, real progress had been made. The government lifted the ban on the LTTE, prisoners of war were exchanged, and the LTTE dropped its demand for a separate state. In October, the LTTE announced plans to become a democratic party.

British prime minister Tony Blair and Irish leader Bertie Ahern sign the Good Friday Agreement in April, 1998. Although the agreement was broadly welcomed in Northern Ireland, some of its terms have been controversial, including the release of former terrorists from prison.

What can the United Nations do?

To tackle global terror, global solutions are required. The United Nations (UN), an organization of countries set up in 1945 to promote world peace, has played a big role in getting international agreement between countries on how to counter terrorism.

Between 1963 and 2001, the UN passed 12 antiterrorism resolutions, each one addressing a different kind of terrorist activity, including assassination, hostage-taking, bombings, and hijackings. Countries who signed up to these resolutions were obliged to introduce security measures to help prevent such attacks in the future. Resolutions were also passed placing greater restrictions on the movement of terrorist assets, fundraising, and weapons acquisition.

Not all member states signed up to these resolutions. One of the main obstacles was the lack of an internationally agreed definition of terrorism. Several Middle Eastern, African, and Asian countries have argued that people who struggle to liberate themselves from foreign oppression have the right to use all methods available, including force.

However, in the wake of the devastating September 11th attacks, representatives of almost every country in the world gathered at the United Nations headquarters in New York to condemn terrorism. There was also a much greater willingness to sign up to UN resolutions. Ratifications (formal confirmation) of the 12 major resolutions rose by 15 percent.

New York mayor Rudolf Giuliani addresses a special session of the United Nations as part of a five-day debate on terrorism between the 189 member nations.

US president George W. Bush (left) and the secretary-general of the United Nations Kofi Annan visit the remains of the World Trade Center in November, 2001. The government wanted the world to see the devastation caused by the September 11th attacks in order to gather support for its war on terror.

UN action since September 11th

Following the terrorist attacks on September 11, 2001, the United Nations passed Resolution 1373. It obliged states to take a number of measures, which included criminalizing the fundraising activities of terrorists, freezing the financial assets of terrorist groups, and exchanging information about known terrorist groups. The Resolution also set up a Counter-terrorism Committee with the job of looking at the counter-terrorism legislation in each member state and identifying areas where this legislation could be improved.

The United Nations has a number of agencies that specialize in different areas of counter-terrorism. These include the International Atomic Energy Agency, which develops measures to protect nuclear facilities and materials from terrorist activity. Another agency, the International Civil Aviation Organization, looks at ways of improving security on commercial flights, such as its March, 2002 resolution to reinforce cockpit doors, making it harder for terrorists to hijack planes.

Sometimes, the UN has imposed sanctions on states that sponsor terrorism. These can call upon members to suspend diplomatic relations with the offending country, or to cease trading with it. UN sanctions were put in place against Libya in 1988 after the bombing of Pan Am flight 103 by Libyan-backed terrorists, and against Sudan in 1995 following the attempted assassination of President Mubarak of Egypt by terrorists based in Sudan.

Does the UN make a difference?

The impact of the UN on terrorism is difficult to measure. It lacks the power by itself to enforce its resolutions. Nevertheless, it plays a valuable role in coordinating the counter-terrorism policies of many different countries. The support of the UN gives states the authority to take firm action against terrorists, on their own, or together.

DEBATE—Is military action the only possible response to terrorism?

- Yes. If governments negotiate with terrorists, it will act as a message to all terrorists, now and in the future, that violence works.
- No. Killing people only creates new martyrs, and sends a government on a downward spiral of ever-increasing repressiveness. The only lasting solution to terrorist conflict is negotiation.

In November, 2002, US forces launched a missile attack on a car in Yemen, killing six al Qaeda members. The missile was launched from a Predator unmanned aircraft, such as the one pictured below. The advanced technology used in this strike illustrates the ability of modern states to target terrorists in remote locations.

Is military action a solution?

The first instinct of many governments is to confront terrorism with force. It is far easier to view terrorism as any other form of violent activity, like crime, and to treat it as a matter for the police or the army. Governments would usually prefer to see terrorism this way than as a reflection of their own unjust policies.

Military action, however, is not as straightforward a solution as it first appears. Terrorist groups are usually well hidden, and made up of self-contained cells. Each cell receives its instructions from an intermediary (middle person). They have little or no contact with other cells or the overall leadership. Because of this dispersed structure, the successful destruction of one or more cells can still leave the organization intact.

Abu Jihad, the PLO's military leader, was assassinated by Israeli forces in Tunisia in 1987. The Israeli government has always claimed the right to assassinate its enemies.

Assassination

Many experts agree that international law allows the assassination of terrorist leaders, because as "illegal combatants" they do not enjoy the protection of international law. Several states have used assassination as a weapon against terrorism. In the 1990s, the US government authorized the assassination of Osama bin Laden [not yet achieved]. Israel authorized the assassination of the Palestinians involved in the killing of Israeli athletes at the 1972 Munich Olympics. In 1996, Yahya Ayyash, a bomb designer working for Hamas, was killed by Israeli agents.

What is the role of covert action?

Governments are therefore obliged to adopt covert (undercover) methods in dealing with terrorism. These can include attempts at infiltrating terrorist organizations, freezing its assets, or cutting off its funding. Some governments are tempted to introduce repressive measures in order to stamp out a terrorist threat. They may decide to introduce a system of identity cards, which people are required by law to carry, to be better informed about the population. They may use surveillance on suspected terrorists, arrest on suspicion of a crime, imprisonment without trial, even torture. Tough tactics like these affect the rights and freedoms of everyone, including innocent civilians. This approach can play into the terrorists' hands by causing people to turn against the government and start to sympathize with the terrorist cause.

Occasionally, military action is taken against states that sponsor terrorism. In 1986, the US government launched military air strikes against Libya. This operation was in response to the bombing of a West Berlin disco, which killed two American servicemen. The air strikes were widely seen as an attempt to assassinate the Libyan leader, Colonel Muammar Qaddafi.

Why did the "War on Terror" start?

The terrorist attacks on September 11, 2001 shocked the world. In a carefully coordinated plan, four American planes were hijacked on the same morning. Two were flown into the World Trade Center in New York, another was flown into the Pentagon in Washington D.C., and a fourth crashlanded in Pennsylvania. More than 3,000 people lost their lives that day.

Within days of the attacks, President George W. Bush announced that the US would wage a "War on Terror." Their first target would be al Qaeda, the organization almost certainly responsible for the attacks. Al Qaeda had its base in Afghanistan, where it enjoyed the support and protection of the Islamic fundamentalist regime, the Taliban.

Within weeks, the US had assembled a coalition of about 40 nations. Many of these countries offered active support in the War on Terror, ranging from the sharing of intelligence or military facilities, to full-scale military assistance. In October, after the Taliban refused to hand over the al Qaeda leader, Osama bin Laden, air strikes were launched.

Within two months, the Taliban was overthrown by a combination of US and British bombing, and ground attacks by the Afghan opposition forces, the Northern Alliance. Al Qaeda bases in mountainous eastern Afghanistan continued to be attacked until mid-2002, and many were destroyed, but bin Laden and other al Qaeda leaders eluded capture.

One of the hijacked planes about to smash into the south tower of the World Trade Center on September 11, 2001. Smoke pours out of the gaping hole in the north tower from the earlier collision. Both towers collapsed shortly afterward.

When will it end?

The US administration warned that the War on Terror could last years, possibly decades. It would be fought on several fronts. As well as military force against terrorists and those who harbored them, less visible forms of action would be taken. Diplomatic and economic pressure would be placed on countries suspected of supporting terrorism. Terrorist assets would be frozen, and pressure would be placed on the global banking system to prevent the movement of terrorist funds.

Modern terrorism

In a speech on November 12, 2002, British Prime Minister, Tony Blair, spelled out the dangers of modern terrorism. "...today's breed of terrorist knows no bounds—of geography, of inhumanity, or of scale. They are looking for ever more dramatic and devastating outrages to inflict upon the people they claim to be their enemy. There is this added dimension; it is not just that they care nothing for the lives of others, they care nothing for the loss of their own life."

A year after the attacks, over a hundred million dollars of terrorist assets had been frozen, and bank accounts had been blocked in over 160 countries. Despite this, a UN report warned that al Qaeda's finances remained healthy. Despite the break-up of its bases and training camps in Afghanistan, the US estimated that al Qaeda continued to have cells in around 60 countries.

In October 2002, al Qaeda proved it remained a formidable threat with three attacks connected to it. On October 6, the French supertanker *Limburg* was attacked off the coast of Yemen. Six days later came the bomb attack on a Bali nightclub that killed more than 180 and, on October 24, Chechen rebels seized a Moscow theater, taking more than 700 people hostage.

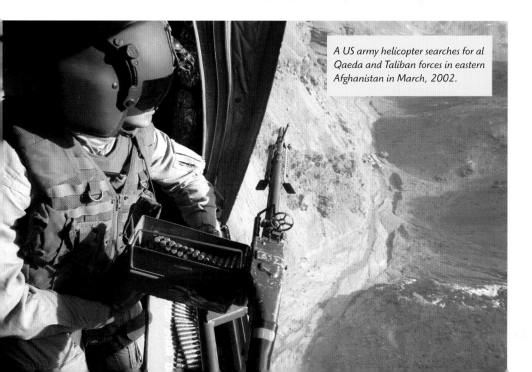

A US army helicopter searches for al Qaeda and Taliban forces in eastern Afghanistan in March, 2002.

How can states protect us?

To protect themselves from future acts of terrorism, states must take steps to improve their security. To do this, they will need to tighten up border and transportation security; be ready to deal with terrorist attacks when they arise, including attacks by weapons of mass destruction; and improve their intelligence-gathering systems to try to prevent future terrorist attacks before they occur.

Checks at land borders, ports, and airports in countries targeted by terrorists have been made stricter since September 11th. Hand luggage at many airports is limited to one bag, and any sharp implements found in hand luggage are confiscated. A computer-screening program is used at American airports to identify passengers who may pose a security risk. On airplanes, there have been moves to strengthen cockpit doors, to include more plainclothes sky marshals (armed officers), and to train flight crews on how to deal with a hijacking.

Terrorist attacks involving WMD are potentially the most difficult to guard against. A bioterrorist attack, for example, would be hard to detect. It could go unnoticed until victims began to get sick and visit hospitals, at which point an unusual trend might be noticed. Hospitals can prepare for a bioterrorist attack by having well-trained staff vaccinated against a range of likely biological agents, preparing isolation wards, and keeping a stockpile of necessary drugs and vaccines.

In the event of a chemical attack, such as a bomb at a chemical plant, police, firefighters, and paramedics, wearing protective suits and gas masks, would establish a cordon around the scene. They would try to decontaminate victims, who would then be sent to nearby hospitals for further care. In a radiation attack, victims would also need to be decontaminated. Radioactive dust would need to be prevented from spreading, as this could contaminate food and water supplies.

An armed policeman on patrol at Heathrow Airport in the UK in October, 2001. Since September 11th, security has become much tighter in airports around the world.

Governments can also help prevent future terrorist attacks by improving their intelligence about terrorists operating within their country and abroad. Governments collect vast amounts of data every day, such as visa application interviews, tax returns, police investigations, and intelligence reports. This information, if cross-checked, could provide vital clues to future terrorist attacks. However, some fear that the use of this information for counter-terrorism could end up affecting the rights and freedoms of ordinary people. It could be used, for example, to monitor the activities of law-abiding people who publicly criticize government policy.

A remote-control bomb disposal robot examines a suspect suitcase in Belgium in December, 2001. New technology such as this can help in the fight against terrorism.

What can we do?

On an individual level, we can also take action to protect ourselves, and others, from the threat of terrorism. We can be more vigilant (aware) when in the street, at school or at work, and while traveling abroad. For example, an unattended package in an airport or on a train should always be reported. Terrorism is certain to be a threat for many years to come, and in a war against terrorism, everyone is on the front line.

DEBATE—Would compulsory identity cards help to protect us against terrorism?

* Yes. They would enable authorities to identify terrorists more easily.
* No. Identity cards can be stolen and false identities can be created by sophisticated terrorists. Identity cards are also an infringement on our rights.

REFERENCE

TERRORIST ORGANIZATIONS

A glossary of the top terrorist organizations operating in the world today, with brief information about each one.

ORGANIZATION	TYPE	ACTIVITIES	STRENGTH	LOCATION
Abu Nidal Organization (ANO)	Islamic fundamentalist	Attacks in 20 countries including US, UK, France, Israel.	A few hundred	Iraq and Lebanon
Abu Sayyaf Group (ASG)	Islamic fundamentalist	Kidnappings, bombings, assassinations.	Around 1,000	Philippines and Malaysia
Al-Aqsa Martyrs Brigade	Palestinian nationalist	Shootings and suicide bombings in Israel.	Unknown	West Bank
Armed Islamic Group (GIA)	Islamic fundamentalist	Assassinations, car bombs, kidnappings of government workers, civilians, and foreigners.	Around 200	Algeria
Asbat al-Ansar	Islamic fundamentalist	Assassinations of religious leaders, bombings of nightclubs, theaters, liquor stores.	Around 300	Lebanon
Aum Supreme Truth, Aum Shinrikyo, Aleph	Religious cult	Best known for sarin gas attack on Tokyo subway (1995). Changed name to Aleph in Jan., 2000 and claims to have rejected violence.	1,500–2,000	Japan and Russia
Basque Fatherland and Liberty (ETA)	Basque nationalist	Bombings and assassinations of Spanish government, military, and judicial figures.	Several hundred	Basque regions of Spain
Al-Gama'a al-Islamiyya (Islamic Group, IG)	Islamic fundamentalist	Armed attacks on Egyptian government figures, plus tourists.	Unknown	Egypt
Hamas (Islamic Resistance Movement)	Islamic fundamentalist	Large-scale suicide bomb attacks on Israel.	Unknown	West Bank, Gaza Strip
Harakat ul-Mujahidin (HUM) (Movement of Holy Warriors)	Islamic fundamentalist	Attacks on Indian troops and civilians, plus a hijacking (1999).	Several thousand	Pakistan
Hezbollah (Party of God)	Islamic fundamentalist	Numerous anti-US and anti-Israeli attacks, including suicide truck bomb (1983) and hijacking (1985).	Several thousand	Lebanon
Islamic Movement of Uzbekistan (IMU)	Islamic fundamentalist	Car bombs, hostage taking, aimed at Uzbekistani government and foreigners.	Probably under 2,000	Throughout South Asia and Tajikistan
Jaish-e-Mohammed (JEM) (Army of Mohammed)	Islamic fundamentalist	Bomb attacks, hijackings, kidnappings against Indian and Western interests.	Several hundred	Peshawar, Muzaffarabad, Kashmir
Al-Jihad (Egyptian Islamic Jihad)	Islamic fundamentalist	Assassinations of Egyptian govt members, car bombings against US and Egyptian facilities.	Probably several hundred	Yemen, Lebanon Afghanistan, Pakistan, UK
Kahane Chai (Kach)	Jewish fundamentalist	Harassment of and threats against Palestinians in West Bank & Gaza.	Unknown	Israel and West Bank
Kurdistan Workers' Party (PKK)	Kurd nationalist	Attacks against Turkish govt, bombings of tourist sites, and kidnapping of tourists.	4–5,000	Turkey, Europe, Middle East

Organization	Type	Activities	Strength	Location
Lashkar-e-Tayyiba (LT) (Army of the Righteous)	Islamic fundamentalist	Attacks against Indian troops and civilian targets.	Several hundred	Muridke and Muzaffarabad, Pakistan
Liberation Tigers of Tamil Eelam (LTTE)	Tamil nationalist	Assassinations and bombings aimed at Sri Lankan political and military leaders.	8–10,000	Northern and eastern coastal Sri Lanka
Mujahedin-e Khalq Organization (MEK or MKO)	Islamic fundamentalist and communist	Worldwide campaign against Iranian government and Western interests in Iran.	Several thousand	Iraq
National Liberation Army (ELN) Colombia	Communist	Kidnapping, hijacking, bombing, guerrilla war. Attacks foreign interests and energy infrastructure.	3–5,000	Rural north-east and south-west Colombia
Palestine Islamic Jihad (PIJ)	Islamic fundamentalist	Large-scale suicide bombings against Israeli military and civilian targets.	Unknown	Israel, West Bank, Gaza Strip
Palestine Liberation Front (PLF)	Palestinian nationalist	Aerial attacks against Israel.	Unknown	Iraq
Popular Front for the Liberation of Palestine (PFLP)	Palestinian nationalist	Attacks against Israeli or moderate Arab targets.	Around 800	Syria, Lebanon, West Bank, Gaza
Popular Front for the Liberation of Palestine-General Command (PFLP-GC)	Palestinian nationalist	Guerrilla operations in southern Lebanon, small-scale attacks on Israel, West Bank and Gaza.	Several hundred	Syria, Lebanon
Al Qaeda	Islamic fundamentalist	Large-scale attacks against US interests worldwide. Responsible for Sept. 11 attacks on US homeland.	Several thousand	Cells in about 60 countries
Real IRA (RIRA)	Irish nationalist	Bombings, assassinations, robberies. Targets include British military and Protestant community.	100–200	Northern Ireland, UK
Revolutionary Armed Forces of Colombia (FARC)	Communist	Bombings, murder, kidnapping, hijacking, and guerrilla warfare against Colombian political, military and economic targets.	9–12,000	Colombia, Venezuela, Panama, Ecuador
Revolutionary Nuclei	Communist	Arson attacks and bombings against American, Greek, and European targets in Greece.	Unknown, but small	Athens, Greece
Revolutionary Organization 17 November (17 November)	Communist	Assassinations of US officials and Greek public figures. Bombings of EU facilities and foreign businesses.	Unknown, but small	Athens, Greece
Revolutionary People's Liberation Party/Front (DHKP/C)	Communist	Attacks against Turkish security and military figures and against foreign interests.	Unknown	Turkey
Sendero Luminoso (Shining Path, or SL)	Communist	Large-scale bombings and assassinations against Peruvian political and military targets.	About 200	Rural Peru
United Self-Defense Forces/Group of Colombia (AUC)	Anti-communist	Assassinations and guerrilla warfare against Colombian communist terrorist groups.	6–8,000	Antioquia, Cordoba, Sucre, and Bolivar, Colombia

Source: Patterns of Global Terrorism, 2001. Published by the Office of the Coordinator of Counterterrorism, US Department of State, May 2002.

TERRORIST ATTACKS

The following table is a chronological list of terrorist attacks that occurred between 1988 and 2002, involving a hundred or more casualties.

DATE	ORGANIZATION RESPONSIBLE	LOCATION	CASUALTIES	DETAILS
10/4/88	Unknown	Islamabad, Pakistan	Killed: 93 Injured: 1,000	Bomb in ammunition dump.
12/21/88	Unknown (Libyan terrorists involved)	Lockerbie, Scotland	Killed: 270 Injured: 0	Bomb on board Pan Am flight 103.
9/19/89	Unknown (Libyan terrorists involved)	Sahara, Niger	Killed: 171 Injured: 0	Bomb on board French aircraft.
11/27/89	The Extraditables, a drug trafficking group	Bogota, Colombia	Killed: 107 Injured: 0	Bomb on board Colombian aircraft.
3/17/92	Hezbollah	Buenos Aires, Argentina	Killed: 29 Injured: 242	Car bomb demolished Israeli embassy.
8/26/92	Unknown	Algiers Airport, Algeria	Killed: 12 Injured: 128	Bomb exploded at ticket counter.
2/26/93	Jihad Group / Al Qaeda	New York City	Killed: 6 Injured: 1,000	Van bomb in underground garage of World Trade Center.
2/25/94	Jewish extremist, Baruch Goldstein	Hebron, West Bank	Killed: 29 Injured: 100	Goldstein opened fire on worshipers in a mosque.
6/27/94	Aum Shinrikyo	Matsumoto, Japan	Killed: 7 Injured: 270	Sarin gas sprayed in residential area.
7/18/94	Hezbollah	Buenos Aires, Argentina	Killed: 100 Injured: 200	Car bomb on Israeli-Argentine Mutual Association.
3/20/95	Aum Shinrikyo	Tokyo, Japan	Killed: 12 Injured: 5,000	Canisters of sarin gas released in subway.
4/19/95	Timothy McVeigh (associated with right-wing militia movement)	Oklahoma City	Killed: 168 Injured: 500	Homemade bomb in van outside Alfred P Murrah federal building.
8/21/95	Hamas	Jerusalem, Israel	Killed: 4 Injured: 100	Suicide bomb in bus.
1/31/96	LTTE	Colombo, Sri Lanka	Killed: 90 Injured: 1,400	Explosives-laden truck rammed in city center.
2/9/96	IRA	London, UK	Killed: 2 Injured: 100	Bomb in Docklands garage.
2/25/96	Hamas	Jerusalem, Israel	Killed: 26 Injured: 80	Suicide bomb in bus.
6/15/96	IRA	Manchester, UK	Killed: 0 Injured: 206	Truck bomb in shopping centre.
6/25/96	Hezbollah / Al Qaeda joint operation suspected	Dharan, Saudi Arabia	Killed: 19 Injured: 515	Truck bomb outside US military facility.
3/30/97	Unknown	Phnom Penh, Cambodia	Killed: 16 Injured: 100	Hand grenade attack on anti-government demonstration.
7/30/97	Hamas	Jerusalem, Israel	Killed: 16 Injured: 178	Two suicide bombings in marketplace.
9/4/97	Hamas	Jerusalem, Israel	Killed: 8 Injured: 200	Three suicide bombings in shopping center.

DATE	ORGANIZATION RESPONSIBLE	LOCATION	CASUALTIES	DETAILS
10/15/97	LTTE	Colombo, Sri Lanka	Killed: 18 Injured: 110	Truck bomb near hotel and World Trade Center.
2/14/98	Islamic militants	Coimbatore, India	Killed: 43 Injured: 200	Series of car bombs in city.
3/5/98	LTTE	Colombo, Sri Lanka	Killed: 36 Injured: 257	Minibus filled with explosives blown up by suicide bomber.
8/7/98	Al Qaeda	Nairobi, Kenya	Killed: 254 Injured: 5,000	Car bomb outside US embassy.
8/15/98	Real IRA	Omagh, Northern Ireland	Killed: 55 Injured: 530	Two car bombs in shopping street.
10/18/98	ELN	Antioquia Department, Colombia	Killed: 71 Injured: 100	Bomb on oil pipeline causing fire.
11/3/98	FARC	Mitu, Colombia	Killed: 138 Injured: 30	Missile attack on police barracks.
3/19/99	Unknown	Vladikavkaz, Russia	Killed: 60 Injured: 100	Bomb in open-air market.
9/4/99	Dagestan or Chechen Islamic group suspected	Buinaksk, Dagestan, Russia	Killed: 64 Injured: 66	Car bomb destroyed military apartment block.
9/9/99	Dagestan or Chechen Islamic group suspected	Moscow, Russia	Killed: 94 Injured: 150	Bomb destroyed apartment building.
9/19/99	Dagestan or Chechen Islamic group suspected	Moscow, Russia	Killed: 118 Injured: 150	Bomb destroyed apartment building.
9/16/99	Dagestan or Chechen Islamic group suspected	Volgodonsk, Russia	Killed: 17 Injured: 100	Truck bomb destroyed apartment building.
8/8/00	Dagestan or Chechen Islamic group suspected	Moscow, Russia	Killed: 7 Injured: 93	Bomb in underground pedestrian walkway.
10/30/00	Hamas	Jerusalem, Israel	Killed: 15 Injured: 130	Suicide bomb in pizza restaurant.
12/25/00	Unknown	Indonesia	Killed: 14 Injured: 100	Around 20 bomb attacks in churches across the country.
5/18/01	Hamas	Netanya, Israel	Killed: 6 Injured: 100	Suicide bomb in shopping mall.
6/1/01	Hamas	Tel-Aviv, Israel	Killed: 20 Injured: 120	Suicide bomb in nightclub.
8/9/01	Hamas	Jerusalem, Israel	Killed: 15 Insured: 130	Suicide bomb in pizza restaurant.
9/11/01	Al Qaeda	New York, Washington D.C., Pennsylvania	Killed: 3,000 Injured: 250	4 hijacked planes were flown into various buildings or crashed.
12/1/01	Hamas	Jerusalem, Israel	Killed: 11 Injured: 188	2 suicide bombings in pedestrian mall.
3/27/02	Hamas	Netanya, Israel	Killed: 29 Injured: 150	Suicide bomb in dining room of hotel.
4/12/02	Martyrs of al-Aqsa	Jerusalem, Israel	Killed: 6 Injured: 100	Suicide bomb in open-air market.
5/10/02	Islamic militants suspected	Kaspiisk, Dagestan	Killed: 40 Injured: 150	Bomb on main street during parade.
9/24/02	Islamic militants suspected	Gujarat, India	Killed: 30 Injured: 70	Gunmen opened fire in Hindu temple.

Date	Organization Responsible	Location	Casualties	Details
9/28/02	Islamic militants suspected	Satkhira, Bangladesh	Killed: 10 Injured: 200	Bomb in movie theater and two bombs in stadium.
10/12/02	Islamic militants suspected	Bali, Indonesia	Killed: 182 Injured: 250	Two car bombs outside popular nightclubs.
10/17/02	Abu Sayyaf or Islamic Liberation Front suspected	Zamboanga, Philippines	Killed: 5 Injured: 100	Two bombs in a department store.
10/26/02	Chechen militant group	Moscow, Russia	Killed: 117 Injured: 650	Hostages held in theater killed by gas poison during rescue operation.

Source: Terror Attack Database, *published by the International Policy Institute for Counter-Terrorism.*

NUMBER OF TERRORIST ATTACKS (1981–2001)

YEAR	2001	2000	1999	1998	1997	1996	1995	1994	1993	1992	1991	1990	1989	1988	1987	1986	1985	1984	1983	1982	1981
NO. OF ATTACKS	348	426	395	274	304	296	440	322	431	363	565	437	375	605	666	612	635	565	498	487	489

Source: Patterns of Global Terrorism, 2001. *Published by the Office of the Coordinator of Counterterrorism, US Department of State, May, 2002.*

NUMBER OF TERRORIST ATTACKS BY REGION (1996–2001)

REGION/YEAR	1996	1997	1998	1999	2000	2001
Africa	11	11	21	53	55	33
Asia	11	21	49	72	98	68
Eurasia	24	42	14	35	31	3
Latin America	84	128	111	122	192	194
Middle East	45	37	31	26	20	29
North America	0	13	0	2	0	4
Western Europe	121	52	48	85	30	17

Source: Patterns of Global Terrorism, 2001. *Published by the Office of the Coordinator of Counterterrorism, US Department of State, May, 2002.*

NUMBER OF CASUALTIES OF TERRORISM BY REGION (1996–2001)

REGION/YEAR	1996	1997	1998	1999	2000	2001
Africa	80	28	5,379	185	102	150
Asia	1,507	344	635	690	898	651
Eurasia	20	27	12	8	103	0
Latin America	18	11	195	9	20	6
Middle East	1,097	480	68	31	78	513
North America	0	7	0	0	0	3,315
Western Europe	503	17	405	16	4	20

Source: Patterns of Global Terrorism, 2001. *Published by the Office of the Coordinator of Counterterrorism, US Department of State, May, 2002.*

FURTHER INFORMATION

BIBLIOGRAPHY

Terrorism Today by Christopher Harmon (Frank Cass, 2000)

Inside Terrorism by Bruce Hoffman (Victor Gollancz, 1998)

How Did This Happen? Terrorism and the New War by James Hoge and Gideon Rose (eds.) (Public Affairs, 2001)

The New Face of Terrorism: Threats from Weapons of Mass Destruction by Nadine Gurr and Benjamin Cole (Tauris, 2000)

Terror in the Mind of God: The Global Rise of Religious Violence by Mark Juergensmeyer (University of California Press, 2000)

States of Terror: Democracy and Political Violence by Peter Taylor (Penguin, 1993)

Points of View: Terrorism by Alison Jamieson (Wayland, 1991)

International Terrorism by Charles W. Kegley (ed.) (St Martin's Press, 1990)

Terrorism: How The West Can Win by Benjamin Netanyahu (ed.) (Avon, 1986)

BOOKS

21st Century Debates: Terrorism by Alex Woolf (Hodder Wayland, 2003)

Why Are People Terrorists? by Alex Woolf (Hodder Wayland, 2003)

Ideas of the Modern World: Fundamentalism by Alex Woolf (Hodder Wayland, 2003)

What's At Issue: War and Conflict by Sean Connolly (Heinemann Library, 2002)

Troubled World: The Troubles in Northern Ireland by Ivan Minnis (Heinemann Library, 2002)

Troubled World: The Arab-Israeli Conflict by Ivan Minnis (Heinemann Library, 2001)

Lives in Crisis: Conflict in Northern Ireland by R. G. Grant (Hodder Wayland, 2001)

Ideas of the Modern World: Communism by Nigel Richie (Hodder Wayland, 2000)

WEBSITES

www.terrorismanswers.com
General information about terrorism in a question-and-answer format.

www.terrorism.com
Essays, profiles of terrorist groups, counter-terrorism documents, and much more from the Terrorism Research Center.

www.terrorismlibrary.com
Links to the websites of newspapers, TV networks, political and academic institutions, with all the latest news and analysis on terrorism and counter-terrorism.

www.fas.org/irp/threat/terror.htm
FAS (Federation of American Scientists) Intelligence Resource Program: Terrorism Intelligence Threat Assessments. Information about counter-terrorist activity since September 11, 2001.

www.fas.org/irp/world
FAS Intelligence Resource Program: Liberation Movements and Terrorist Organizations.
Profiles of counter-terrorist organizations around the world.

www.ict.org.il
The website of an Israeli research institute (the International Policy Institute for Counter Terrorism) containing information and analysis on international terrorism and counter-terrorism.

GLOSSARY

abortion The removal of a human offspring in its early stages of development from a woman's womb in order to end a pregnancy.

anarchist Someone who rejects the need for a government and supports its abolition.

anthrax Bacterial disease of mammals, especially cattle and sheep, transmittable to humans through inhalation, digestion, or cuts in the skin.

bacteria Microorganisms responsible for many plant and animal diseases.

blackmail The act of forcing someone to do something by threatening them in some way.

bubonic plague A highly infectious and fatal disease transmitted by fleas that have bitten an infected host.

capitalism An economic system characterized by a free competitive market and based on private ownership of the means of production.

censorship The suppression of a publication considered offensive or a threat to security.

chlorine gas A heavy, greenish-yellow gas that can be used as a chemical weapon.

cocaine An illegal addictive drug obtained from the leaves of the coca plant.

colonial Relating to a colony, which is a country or territory ruled by another country.

communism A system, or the belief in a system, in which capitalism is overthrown and control of wealth and property resides with the state.

counterfeit Something made as a copy of something else, especially money, to deceive people.

electromagnetic bomb Any device that can produce an electromagnetic field (a field of force associated with a moving electric charge) of such intensity that targeted computer systems are damaged or destroyed.

encryption The conversion of text or computer data into a code to prevent unauthorized people from gaining access to it.

ethnic minority A group with a similar cultural background that forms a minority in a country.

fundamentalism A religious movement based on a strict interpretation of holy writings.

hacking To manipulate a computer in order to gain unauthorized access to files.

heroin An illegal addictive drug obtained from morphine. Morphine is obtained from opium poppies.

homophobia Hatred or fear of homosexuality.

imam A man who leads the prayers in a mosque.

incursion A brief, hostile invasion of another country's territory.

mustard gas An oily liquid, made from ethene and disulfur dichloride, that evaporates to a poison gas.

paramedic Somebody trained to perform emergency medical procedures in the absence of a doctor.

pornography Sexually explicit films, magazines, photographs, and other materials.

propaganda Publicity intended to make people believe something.

radiation Energy emitted in the form of particles by substances, such as uranium and plutonium, whose atoms are not stable and are spontaneously decaying.

repressive Exerting strict control over the freedom of others.

sanctions Measures taken by one or more nations to apply pressure on another nation to conform to international law or opinion, for example, ceasing to trade with it.

self-martyrdom Killing oneself for one's beliefs.

sky marshal An armed officer whose job is to prevent or deal with hijackings.

smallpox A highly contagious disease caused by a pox virus and marked by high fever and the formation of scar-producing pustules.

surveillance Continued observation of a person or group.

totalitarian Relating to a centralized government system in which a single party controls all political, economic, social, and cultural life.

vaccine A preparation containing weakened or dead microbes of the kind that cause a particular disease, administered to stimulate the immune system to produce a resistance to the disease.

VX An oily, liquid, highly lethal, nerve gas.

INDEX

Jordan 11, 28

Kaczynski, Theodore 34
Kahane, Rabbi Meir 18
Kenya 19
Khaled, Leila 12
Khomeini, Ayatollah 28
Kosovo Liberation Army 31
Kurdistan 29

Lebanon 18, 28, 29, 33
left-wing terrorists 16, 24, 30
Lenin 16
Libya 26, 28, 29, 41, 43
loan-sharking 26
Lockerbie 28

Macedonians 9
Mao 16
Marighela, Carlos 22
Marx 16
McCarthy, John 33
McKinley, William 9
McVeigh, Timothy 19, 33
media 20, 21, 24
Meinhof, Ulrike 13
money laundering 26, 31
Moscow 21, 45
Mountbatten, Lord 20
mujahideen 7
Muslims 18, 25, 27
mustard gas 37, 55

Nairobi, Kenya 25
narcoterrorism 31
Narodnaya Volya 9
National Liberation Army 28
Nationaler Widerstand 17
nationalist terrorism 14, 15, 38
Nazi Germany 9
Nazis 17
NDP 17

neo-Nazis 17
Netanyahu, Benjamin 21
North Korea 29
Northern Ireland 15, 25, 32, 39
nuclear weapons 36, 37

Oklahoma City bombing 33
Omagh, Northern Ireland 25, 32
organized crime 26, 30, 31
Ottoman Empire 9

Pakistan 30
Palestine 10, 11, 14, 18, 23
Palestinians 5, 6, 15, 43
    intifada 33
    terrorists 12, 25, 26, 27, 29
Pentagon 22, 44
Peru 5, 16, 27
Pisacane, Carlo 8, 11
PLO 14, 26, 28, 38, 43
plutonium 37, 55
propaganda 8, 21, 55

Qaddafi, Colonel 43

Rabin, Yitzhak 24, 38
racists 17, 19
radiation 37, 46, 55
Real IRA 25
Red Army 16, 28
Red Army Faction 10, 13, 16, 24, 28
Red Brigades 10, 16, 24, 28
Reign of Terror 8
religious terrorists 12, 15, 31
revolutionary terrorism 11
right-wing groups 16, 17, 19, 26, 34
Russia 21
Russian revolutionaries 9

Saudi Arabia 18, 28
self-martyrdom 25, 55
Sendero Luminoso (Shining Path) 5, 16, 27
Sinn Fein 27
smallpox 36, 55
smuggling 26, 30, 37
South America 5, 16
Soviet Union 9, 10, 28, 37
Spain 5, 8
Sri Lanka 14, 35, 39
state-sponsored terrorism 7, 9, 28, 29, 30, 43
student riots 10, 16, 17
Sudan 29, 41
suicide bombs 18, 25, 33
Syria 29

Taliban 44, 45
Tamil Tigers 14, 15, 35, 39
Tanzania 19
Thatcher, Margaret 20, 21
Tokyo, Japan 37
totalitarian regimes 9, 55
Turkey 9, 29

United Nations 40, 41, 45
uranium 37, 55
US State Department 7, 29
Uzbekistan 31

Vietnam 10, 28

War on Terrorism 41, 44, 45
Washington D.C. 19, 22, 44
weapons of mass destruction 36, 46
Weathermen 10, 16
West Bank 6, 14, 18, 27
West Germany 10, 13
World Trade Center 4, 19, 22, 32, 41, 44

Yemen 42, 45